Gladstone Dock in the late 1960s

THE GREAT MERSEY SHIPPING LINES

AS the saying goes, time and tide waits for no man, so as Merseyside moves into a new era with the growing success of the new Liverpool Cruise Terminal, what better time now to take stock of the seeds of this great city by looking back at the Mersey's great shipping Lines, before they slip away in the wake of history . . .

Two phrases were repeatedly voiced by those featured in this book: namely, "they were great times" and "it was like another world".

Opportunities no longer exist to satisfy a desire to get away from the urban drudgery one day and by the next day getting a job on a boat to West Africa, as Graham Austin, of Huyton, relates in these pages.

Unfortunately, teenage boys and girls will never discover with such ease the wonder of overseas people and places – while being paid to do it. This could range from bartering with native parrot sellers 1,000 miles up the Amazon aboard a Booth Line steamer or watching the seals on the St Lawrence ice floes

from the decks of a Canadian Pacific liner.

Speak to any Merseyside seafarer and the memories tumble out, like oddments rolling from the back of a locker in a heavy swell. Steve Grey, of Oxton, was a steward on Shaw Savill's liner Ocean Monarch (ex-Empress of England) and sailed to Japan in 1970 for the international Expo.

"One young lad joined for the six month voyage with a suitcase the size of the Chancellor's red budget box," said Steve.

"At Hong Kong, Chinese tailors boarded the ship, I tried on some trousers which, to the hilarity of my mate, had the seam running across the knees."

However, life is never just plain sailing and also described here are the horrific wartime fates of four teenage "first trippers" aboard Almeda Star and the luckless internees lost on her sister ship Arandora Star.

Times keep moving on. Mass air travel destroyed the ocean liner business, containerisation decimated cargo ship numbers and international conglomerates dispensed with hiring local labour.

That is why it is so important to record the memories of those who were the backbone of the great Mersey merchant fleets which created the very reason for the city's existence, its wealth, employment and fabulous buildings. ➤

➤ This book is no more than a snapshot of the great Liverpool shipping lines, highlighting their various aspects. It is not meant to be a definitive description, but I hope it will bring enjoyment to readers, and stimulate others to get in touch with me at the Liverpool ECHO to relate their maritime memories for our next volume.

Typical of so many seafarers, Chris Brocklehurst, of Platt Bridge, Wigan, had a career which arcs through the great Mersey shipping lines, moving from BP tankers to Cunard White Star's legendary liner Britannic. He wrote: "When the sea is in your blood it never goes away and other seamen will understand that. I'll never regret going to sea."

These pages reek of the pride such people felt about Merseyside – and rightly so - generated by its great shipping lines. Yet this book is not meant solely as sepia memento, it is a bridge between that earlier golden era and the present, as cruise passengers arrive in ever increasing numbers from across Britain to board the new generation of liners.

So climb aboard for not just one, but countless voyages of many lifetimes, as you sail through these stories.

Peter Elson
Liverpool Echo
Shipping Correspondent
January 2013

Cunard

WORLD FAMOUS

Above, the bridge wing of Cunard Line's Caronia. Right, young crew aboard Blue Funnel Line's Protesilaus. Below, Blue Funnel's Patroclus, at Gladstone Dock

LIFE RINGS
AND LINERS

Mersey Merchant Navy
house flags and life rings in
the Daylight on Industry
Exhibition's Shipping Pavilion,
The Strand, Liverpool, on July
23, 1951.
Left: a £2,000 model of
Gladstone Dock gets
its finishing touches at
the British Industry Fair,
Birmingham, in February, 1939

CONTENTS

Written and compiled by: Peter Elson
Design & Production: Vicky Andrews
Trinity Mirror Image Archive: Brian Johnston

Thanks to the following for sharing their encyclopaedic
knowledge of Mersey shipping and making this book possible:
Sir Michael Bibby, Peter Head, Pat Moran, John Shepherd,
Stuart Wood and Patrick Toosey; also Barrie Youde for his
closing poem. I am also indebted to the following for pictures:
Alan Brown, Bibby Line Group, Lynda Husband (for late Alex
Husband), Merseyside Maritime Museum (including Stewart
Bale Collection), National Trust (E Chambre Hardman), Peter
Davenport Collection, Peter Head Collection, Tom McCarten,
and Wayne Colquhoun Circa 1900 Antiques.

Thanks also to all those who contributed by sharing their
memories. We look forward to hearing more of them and
sharing them in future magazines – to contribute to the Lost
Liverpool archives, email lostliverpool@trinitymirror.com

Trinity Mirror Media

Executive Editor: Ken Rogers
Senior Editor: Steve Hanrahan
Editor: Paul Dove
Senior Art Editor: Rick Cooke
Trinity Mirror Media Marketing Executive: Claire Brown
Sales and Marketing Manager: Elizabeth Morgan
Sales and Marketing Assistant: Karen Cadman

© 2013 Trinity Mirror / Liverpool Post & Echo
All Rights Reserved.

No part of "The Great Mersey Shipping Lines" may be reproduced,
stored in a retrieval system, or transmitted in any form, or by any means,
electronic, mechanical, photocopying, recording or otherwise without the
prior permission in writing of the copyright holders, nor be otherwise
circulated in any form of binding or cover other than in which it is published
and without a similar condition being imposed on the subsequent publisher.

Printed by Buxton Press

ISBN 9781908695451

MERSEY MONARCHS

Liverpool's merchant fleet was at its zenith when reviewed in the river in July, 1913, by King George V and Queen Mary aboard SY Galatea, Mersey Docks & Harbour Board's inspection vessel, second left, with Harrison Line's SS Politician, centre, and Cunard Line's Blue Riband of the Atlantic holder, RMS Mauretania, right

To buy prints of the images in this publication, or any photos in our archive collection, visit www.merseyshop.com/buyaphoto or telephone 0845 300 3021

MERSEYSHOP.com

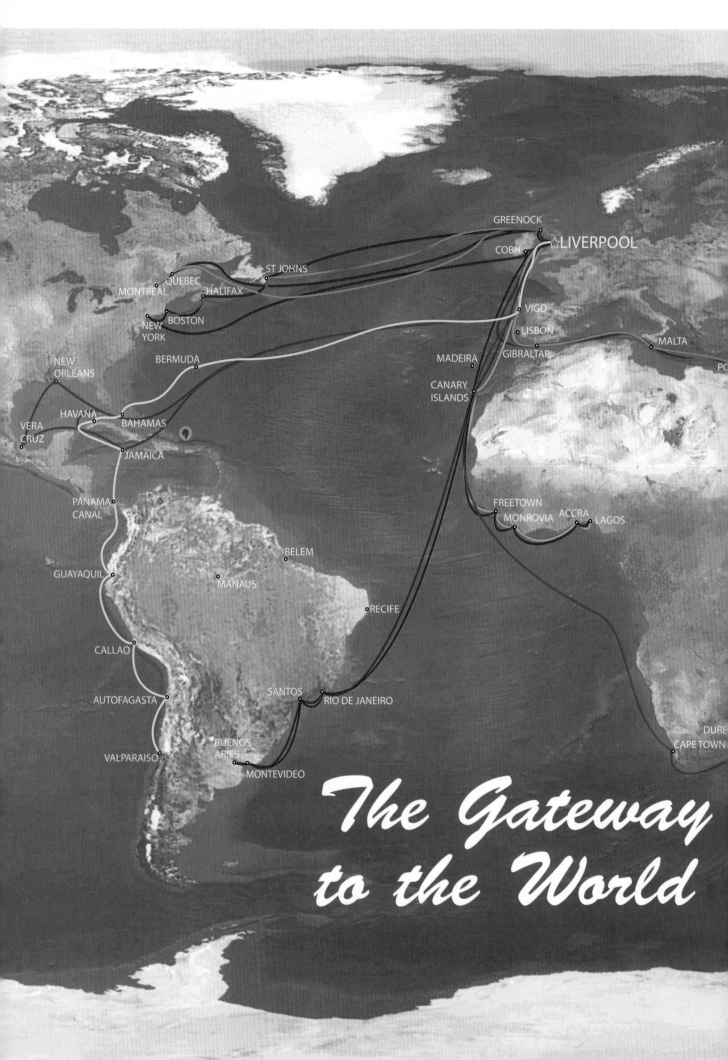

GREENOCK

☆LIVERPOOL

COBH

QUEBEC
MONTREAL
HALIFAX
ST JOHNS
BOSTON
NEW
YORK
BERMUDA
VIGO
LISBON
MALTA
GIBRALTAR
MADEIRA
PO
CANARY
ISLANDS
NEW
ORLEANS
HAVANA
VERA
CRUZ
BAHAMAS
JAMAICA
FREETOWN
MONROVIA
ACCRA
LAGOS
PANAMA
CANAL
BELEM
GUAYAQUIL
MANAUS
RECIFE
CALLAO
AUTOFAGASTA
SANTOS
RIO DE JANEIRO
VALPARAISO
BUENOS
ARIES
MONTEVIDEO
DURE
CAPE TOWN

The Gateway to the World

SHANGHAI

KARACHI

BOMBAY

CALCUTTA

HONG KONG

ADEN

RANGOON

MOGADISHU

OMBASA

ARES
LAAM

SINGAPORE

FREEMANTLE

SYDNEY

PACIFIC STEAM NAVIGATION
CUNARD/ANCHOR LINE
CANADIA PACIFIC
ELDER DEMPSTER
FURNESS
BLUESTAR
BLUE FUNNEL
BIBBY
ELLERMAN
PORT LINE & SHAW SAVILL
HARRISON

ENSURING THE BOATS COME IN

Liverpool piloting in the 1960s

A fine line-up of Liverpool cargo-liners at West Gladstone Dock warehouses with, from left, representatives of Blue Star; MV Adventurer, of Harrison; and Federal Steam Navigation

West Gladstone Dock

STUART WOOD, Liverpool Chief Pilot until 2009 and now a broadcaster on maritime matters is typical of so many Merseysiders.

Brought up in in Wallasey, he joined Brocklebank Line's Martand in 1960.

To build up his sea-going service, he sailed on other now lost lines like Rowbotham's, Booker's and Ellerman & Pappayanni. His pilot apprenticeship ran from 1961-7.

"Initially I was seasick after joining Brocklebanks. Then a wiry Welshman called Taffy Williams told me he was fed up of me doing nothing. We were in the Bay of Biscay and he gave me a bottle of water and a packet of Jacobs crackers and ordered me to get working.

'Well, it cured me and I've never had a problem since."

His father's uncle Bert served on HMS Jervis Bay, the famous armed merchant ship sunk in 1940 by the German warship Admiral Scheer.

He received his pilot's licence (no 172) on his father's birthday on February 14, 1968.

Stuart's career has spanned the end of Liverpool's great liner and traditional cargo ship era into containerisation and high technology.

"I'm thrilled to have lasted long enough to see the liners come back here and bring in the largest passenger ship to visit until then, Grand Princess, last summer.

"When I started there were still lovely liners like Circassia and Cilicia on the India run, Apapa Accra and Aureol for West Africa," he recalls.

"The White Empresses went to Canada, Sylvania went to New York and occasionally we saw the

Liverpool South Docks with Houlder Bros' Queensbury alongside the Brunswick Dock grain silo, and Isle of Man Steam Packet Co's small freighter Peveril, middle centre

great green goddess, Caronia. Mauretania arrived with a black hull for a refit at Laird's and left with a green one to go cruising.

"It was always a thrill to deal with the Elders Fyffes banana boats for obvious reasons. These were beautiful ships carrying a couple of dozen passengers, docking at Garston.

"We used to be given bunches of green bananas and slowly ripen them in the shower. They lasted until the next boat arrived.

"Luckily, no big spiders ever emerged from them."

Canadian Pacific's Atlantic fleet idle in Gladstone Dock after the Wall Street Crash ruined trade; from left: Montclare, Duchesses of Richmond, York and Atholl.

QUARTET

Top, four tugs of two famous towage companies from different eras - steam tug Bangarth, of Rea Towing, and diesel tug Egerton, of Alexandra Towing, with two fleetmates strikebound in Gladstone Dock, February 22, 1968

UP AND AWAY

Left, the heavy lift crane on Ellerman Line's City of Barcelona swings aboard steam locomotives built by Vulcan Foundry, at Newton-le-Willows, Lancashire, probably bound for the Middle East or India

STRUCK AGAIN

Top, another dock strike on October 12, 1967, traps several freighters from Blue Star, Booker, Bank and American Saint Lines, in South Canada Dock

NEW NOVA

The first postwar Furness Withy liner, SS Nova Scotia, 7,500 gross tons, is berthed in Hornby Dock, on August 24, 1947, after trials and prior to her maiden voyage to St John's, Newfoundland; Halifax, Nova, Scotia, and Boston, Mass

The big new Royal Seaforth Dock confirmed the Mersey container age seen here with Atlantic Container Line's ro-ro freighter Atlantic Span, in February, 1982

After grounding in Bermuda, Pacific Steam's flagship MV Reina Del Pacifico is finally home and hugger-mugger with Alexandra's tug tender Flying Breeze, in Gladstone Lock, July 25, 1957

Houlder Bros' freighter Westbury looms over the crew of a Liverpool Victoria Rowing Club eight as they power to victory in the Victoria Cup Race, at the Merseyside Rowing Regatta, in West Float, Birkenhead, in May 1968

Lamey steam tugs Edith Lamey and Margaret Lamey at right angles to Alexandra's venerable namesake tug Alexandra, with Port Line's cargo-liner Port Napier behind

Blue Star Line's white cruise liner Arandora Star off Liverpool Pier Head, with a Wallasey ferry and schooner in Gordon Ellis' beautifully atmospheric painting

INTO THE BLUE

ARANDORA STAR - from deluxe liner to death trap . . .

WARTIME prime minister Winston Churchill's unfortunate phrase "Collar the lot" about ex-patriot Germans and Italians led to fatal consequences.

Long-settled expatriates in Britain or refugees, escaping from the atrocities of Nazi Germany and Austria, were rounded up. Many were interned in a half-finished Huyton council estate.

Particularly ill-fated was the deportation of 479 German and 734 Italian interned men (among a total of 1,673 people) aboard the former super deluxe liner SS Arandora Star, from Liverpool to St Johns, Newfoundland, Canada.

SS Arandora Star, built by Cammell Laird at Birkenhead (like her sistership Almeda Star), was one of the most famous liners of the 1930s. She was one of Blue Star Line's "Luxury Flying Five", built for UK - River Plate service, a company owned by Liverpool's Vestey family, but was rebuilt as one of the world's premier cruise liners.

On June 29, 1940, Arandora Star sailed unescorted from Liverpool and on July 2, at 06.15, while 75 miles off Bloody Foreland, Co Donegal, she was torpedoed by U-47. Mass panic broke out among the internees and they swamped attempts to launch the lifeboats. The ship sank rapidly and it was only through the heroic rescue by the Canadian destroyer St Laurent that 868 people were saved. However, the death toll was 805.

Evan Morgan Jones, from Merthyr Tydfil, was a Welch Regiment soldier, aged 21, and was a guard aboard Arandora Star when the torpedo struck at 6am.

"I was on the back top deck, going down to breakfast and there was this 'boof' sound and the abandon ship alarm sounded," he recalled.

"I told my friend Jackie Powell we'd have to jump. He was terrified as he couldn't swim. I said 'there's plenty of water, you'll soon learn!' ➤

WHITE LADY

Nicknamed "the wedding cake", SS Arandora Star, 14,694 gross tons, built by Cammell Laird, Birkenhead, in 1927, steams down the Mersey. As a deluxe cruise liner she carried 354 passengers, but had 1,600 aboard when torpedoed, on July 2, 1940

➤ "I chucked two loose planks overboard. The ship was moving, but sliding down bow first. It was a 50ft drop, so I pushed Jackie down, then jumped myself."

Arandora Star disappeared within 30 minutes and Evan and Jack, with an arm over each plank, paddled for their lives in the debris field.

Evan said: "I couldn't believe it, but I saw the captain and an officer on the bridge standing to attention as the ship sank. It wasn't so bad in the water as it was summer. Soon the sea filled with broken deckchairs and dead bodies."

The pair were eight hours in the water before spotting a lifeboat and were hauled aboard. They were finally rescued by St Laurent.

Evan said: "It was exhausting as I had to carry Jackie's senses and my own. I come from a big religious family and I felt someone was looking out for me.

"My mother used to worry about me swimming in a valley pool near our house. When I got home, I said to her, 'Now you see what my swimming's done!'."

Rando Bertoia, now 88, was a terrazzo layer when he was taken, aged 20, from his family in Glasgow, the day after Italy declared war.

His father was interned in the Isle of Man, but he said: "I was one of the lucky ones. We were sleeping on deck as it was so warm and I was pushed into a lifeboat. If I'd slept below decks, I wouldn't be here.

"A week later, we were back in Liverpool and on the British India ship Dunera for Australia.

"I don't feel bitter. I was very, very lucky."

The 1948-built Melbourne Star, 13,179 gross tons, unloads the traditional way on May 9, 1972, just before the container revolution finished break-cargo shipments like this

SS Brasil Star, 10,716 gross tons, built by Cammell Laird, Birkenhead, in 1947, enters Sandon Lock, Liverpool and was one of four postwar sisters to replace Blue Star's Flying Five 'A' class all lost in the war

A white-shirted ship's boss instructs his hatch-men on June 20, 1969, to deal with Blue Star Line's MV Iberia Star, 10,894 gross tons with 248 first class passenger capacity, built in 1950 as the Belgian cargo-liner Baudouinville

LOVED ONES LOST AT WAR

Forgotten teenage heroes lost on Almeda Star

A CHANCE remark by Jimmy Kavanagh's elder brother, Tommy, saved the then 13-year-old boy from a terrible death in the North Atlantic.

However, Tommy was not so lucky. As a 15-year-old "first-tripper" cabin boy, he met his untimely end soon afterwards in one of the most mysterious wartime sinkings.

In spite of their young age, both the Kavanagh boys had signed on as crew for the Blue Star Line's SS Almeda Star, due to sail out of Liverpool for Argentina, on December 22, 1941.

But Tommy told his grandmother what they intended to do. She in turn told his father. While he reluctantly allowed Tommy to sail, he regarded Jimmy as too young and made Blue Star Line officials sign him off.

Tommy and three classmates from Florence Melly School, Walton – John Barret, 16, Patrick Gallagher, 16, and Freddy Hall, 17 – embarked on Almeda Star.

All four teenagers had met and agreed to join in the war. With a desperate manpower shortage, Blue Star was not averse to employing them.

While still in the Mersey, Almeda Star was in collision and then bombed, returning twice for repairs.

Tommy remembers his brother returning home with a plaster on his chin, applied by the ship's purser after being injured during the attack.

Almeda Star finally sailed on January 15, 1941, but two days later at 7.45 am was torpedoed by U-96 (the subject of the acclaimed 1981 film Das Boot). A foul storm was raging and the liner sank 350 miles west of the Outer Hebrides.

Inexplicably, no bodies, lifeboats or debris from Almeda Star were ever found. Just one distress call was made from the liner, heard by the US forces coastguard and reported in the British press.

The Admiralty still claim to know nothing about the sinking apart from acknowledging the ship's loss.

As a lasting tribute to his brother's selfless sacrifice, Jimmy Kavanagh, from Eldon Village, Vauxhall, who served 40 years in the Merchant Navy, tried to get an

Two views in the Mersey of Blue Star Line's SS Almeda Star, 14,950 gross tons, of the Flying Five 'A' class, after lengthening in 1935, by Cammell Laird, Birkenhead, where she was built in 1926. While en route from Liverpool to the River Plate all 360 passengers and crew were lost after being torpedoed off Rockall, near the Outer Hebrides, on January 17, 1941

Atlantic Star medal on behalf of his brother, but was rebuffed by the Maritime & Coastguards Agency medals department as his dead sibling did not satisfy the time spent at sea qualifications.

"After we got jobs with Blue Star, we got a lift on a wagon down the Dock Road and boarded Almeda Star. Later, my father went to the ship and stopped me going.

"My brother's loss permanently devastated my family. He was like a twin brother to me, a popular, lovely lad. While Almeda Star was being repaired, my brother was at my grandmother's having dinner, with the plaster on his chin.

"My grandmother said, 'You don't have to go back on that ship. There's plenty of jobs ashore'.

He replied, 'No Nan, I'm going with my mates'. That was the last time I saw him."

The Blue Funnel Line

FUNNEL VISION

Mike Malloy gets an anatomy lesson . . .

SEX education in the 1960s was more haphazard than in these up-front contemporary times.

Michael Malloy, of Vauxhall, was a junior rating and bathroom steward on the Blue Funnel express cargo liner Ixion, on which he made seven voyages to the Far East.

His daily job was to ask the 36 first class passengers when they required a bath, run it and clean it.

"The bathrooms weren't en suite, but were shared between two staterooms and there was a doorway into the passage. Doing my rounds I went in to one as the door sign said 'Vacant'.

"An older lady hadn't locked the door and stood up and started screaming. Obviously, I muttered my apologies and scarpered.

"In case there was a complaint, I told the chief steward who passed it onto his boss who said, 'Seeing a bit of arse won't do the boy any harm'!

"Most of the passengers were wealthy Australians who were nice to deal with. Crossing the Indian Ocean, the crew would put up cricket nets for a deck match.

"One professional Australian player complimented me on my ability and asked where I learned my cricket, I said, 'Under a lamp-post in Carisbrooke Road, Bootle, sir'.

"I loved the freedom of deep sea long voyages and was away once for four months, but even enjoyed round land voyages on Perseus and Pyrrhus from Liverpool to Glasgow.

"I sailed on Menelaus twice and have done seven voyages on the trot. My last voyage was on Peleus in 1968."

RACY

Blue Funnel's handsome new £2.5m MV Centaur, 8,282 gross tons, pulls away from Princes Landing Stage Liverpool, on January 21, 1964, after her only visit. She operated on the Freemantle, Australia - Singapore run, carrying 190 passengers and 4,500 sheep or 700 head of cattle

Five cargo-liners bunched into Alfred Basin, Birkenhead with Blue Funnel's Perseus and Ellerman's City of Winnipeg, centre. Indian Renown is unloading, right and Cock tug's Storm Cock lurks in the foreground. Above, unloading resumes on Sundays at Gladstone Dock, in January, 1964, with Blue Funnel's MV Patroculus, 10,109 gross tons, built in 1950

India Buildings, Alfred Holt & Co's head office for Blue Funnel Line and Elder Dempster Lines at Water Street, built 1924-32

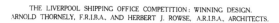

THE LIVERPOOL SHIPPING OFFICE COMPETITION: WINNING DESIGN.
ARNOLD THORNELY, F.R.I.B.A., AND HERBERT J. ROWSE, A.R.I.B.A., ARCHITECTS.

Michael Malloy left school in 1959 and weeks later was an office boy at Holt's Warehouse, Gladstone Dock, aiming to join the Blue Funnel catering department.

This was a stepping stone into the head office for the mighty Alfred Holt & Co at India Buildings, in Water Street (all the lifts had uniformed attendants) and head office of Blue Funnel Line.

"In there was Holt's Rest Room, which had the full gear - soft furnishings and leather chairs. Staff never ate at desks but had a 20 minute break for morning coffee and afternoon tea at the Rest Room," said Mike.

"On the eighth floor was the senior management dining room. Blue Funnel would be on one side of the room, Elder Dempster people on the other.

"Sir John Nicholson, the head of the company, would carve a joint at lunchtime and my job was to take the plates over to a stewardess who put the veg on them, so I could serve the other nine directors, such as George and Julian Holt.

"One day my attention wandered and I was gawping out of the window, to be abruptly startled by Sir John saying, 'Come on, boy, hurry up!' as he'd already filled most of the plates.

"I also had six weeks training at Holt's Odyssey Works in Corporation Road, Birkenhead. Blue Funnel was one of the finest companies to work for and really looked after their staff.

"I also worked for Cunard and Canadian Pacific, but the ships were too big. My best times were with Blue Funnel."

India Buildings' Rest Room for Holt's staff

BOMBAY BEAUTIES

MV Circassia, right, of 1937, 11,157 gross tons, is guided from Birkenhead North Lock, by Alexandra tug North Buoy, in the mid-1960s, and flying the No 5 flag of Anchor Line's appropriated (ie dedicated) pilot Reginald Youde. Gig boatman Henry Cotgrave, of Seacombe, is ready to take the bow line. Sister ship MV Cilicia, main picture, built by Fairfield, of Govan, in 1938, fresh from postwar refurbishment, sets sail on October 2, 1948, flying the new Pakistani national flag on her foremast as Karachi will be the first call on the sub-continent.

ANCHORS AWAY!

THEY weren't the biggest liners in Liverpool, but everyone recalls how the beautiful condition of the Anchor Line postwar passenger motor ships Caledonia, Cilicia and Circassia on the UK - India run.

Barry Ledsham, of Bromborough, explained the liners' schedule: "Inbound from Bombay, it was Princes Landing Stage for passengers, Sandon Dock for freight, then up to Glasgow for turnaround, outbound to East Float, Birkenhead, over to Princes Stage and off to India again."

Pat Moran, of Hesketh Park, said: "Anchor liners were famed for their cuisine, especially curries as they had Indian galley crew.

"The ships themselves were always in pristine condition, as if they'd just left the shipyard."

Colin Woolland, of Eastham, said: "These were Anchor's fast passenger ships, while I was on Eucadia, an intermediate freighter with only 30 passengers. It was a brilliant time."

James Murphy, of Aigburth, said: "They were lovely ships. I worked on Alexandra and Lamey tugs from 1956 and remember these liners. Later I was engine room crew on Cunard's Carinthia to Canada and Sylvania to New York.

"Great times."

SNOWED UP

MV Aureol will soon swap snow for tropical heat after she leaves Princes Landing Stage for West Africa, on February 8, 1969

SNOWED UP

MV Aureol will soon swap snow for tropical heat after she leaves Princes Landing Stage for West Africa, on February 8, 1969

UP THE CREEK

Life as an Elder Dempster trainee manager . . .

Patrick Toosey admires John Stobart's fine painting of MV Aureol, in Merseyside Maritime Museum

ELDER Dempster Lines was the lynch-pin of trade with West Africa. Originally Liverpool merchant adventurers loaded up their boats with all manner of goods to sell to the native tribes. The company started in 1852 and was finally wound-up in 2000, having owned 500 ships in that time.

"Alfred Jones created a regular cargo steam ship service to take out to west Africa whatever was needed and bring back whatever he could find," said Patrick Toosey, of Oxton, an ex-Elder Dempster senior manager and chairman of Elders of Elders, the company's former employees' association.

"There was a big connection with the Canary Islands as this was a major coal-bunkering station. Given the problems of working in the tropics, those employees were tough, tough folks.

"Elders sometimes traded as far as South Africa, but never to the Far East. It's extraordinary how Liverpool developed expanding its worldwide services in the late 18th and 19th centuries.

"The shipping families used to co-operate with one another. Blue Funnel, which ran to the Far East took a share in Elders during the 1920s to help them out financially, although it could never really empathise with the places we worked.

"My father was on the Elders board with the chairman John Joyce, who was a very good businessman but not a good people person. My old man was the opposite and was a great people person.

"After school, I was interviewed by both Blue Funnel and Elder Dempster. Blue Funnel asked what kind of a degree I'd get and I replied I might scrape a second class one. Their response was 'we only have firsts here' – so that was

me written off. In contrast, Elders said we will keep a job open for you after university and to become a management trainee. On this you were batted around Liverpool docks for six months.

"You started at Brunswick and Harrington Docks and constantly had the mick taken out of you by the dockers, but by God you learned what really happened in those departments.

"Any dirty jobs were dumped on you which quickly brought you down to earth."

Patrick's first voyage was in 1954 aboard a 10,000 ton freighter, Mary Kingsley (one of a class named after British missionaries) out to West Africa.

"There was always a bit of accommodation and no air conditioning, but I had the greatest possible time.

"I was paid £1 to be a purser's assistant (basically a clerk) and we ➤

➤ went literally up the creeks, deep into the Niger delta," he said.

"We had someone up on the sharp end swinging the lead and shouting the depth up to the captain on the bridge. The pilots were tribesmen who paddled out in their canoes to get us over the bar.

"Our turnaround was Sapele, which had a huge timber and ply-wood wharf. The ship would be tied up to a tree!"

Once ashore his first job gloried in the name assistant log wharf superintendent at Takoradi, Ghana.

He recalled: "The Ghanaians are the cream of West Africa, Lovely, highly competent people. I was then shuffled along to Accra as passenger manager, as we had three liners and a freighter fleet. Before the quay was built at Accra, passengers were put onto a 'nanny chair' - six either side - and a derrick swung them on and off canoes alongside the ship.

"We never lost one person. Cars were handled the same way, put onto two canoes lashed together get them ashore."

His first trip out to West Africa

WAITING GAME

Boys play cricket at Egremont, while MV Aureol lies at anchor, mid-Mersey, ready to enter the docks to unload (derricks already raised) from West Africa, June 20, 1963

by an Elder Dempster liner was for his honeymoon aboard MV Accra. He said: " We were in the lowest possible accommodation next to steerage. We'd got a twin berth cabin, which isn't what you'd like on your honeymoon.

"Apart from that, it was great fun and there were loads of passengers. The ship was air conditioned, so it felt reasonably comfortable in the heat.

"The crew was a mix of British and African. ED employed a lot of Africans and people were gagging for the jobs as the training was so good."

Sailing out of Liverpool for his second tour of duty in 1956, he travelled "lower first class" aboard the flagship MV Aureol, to become claims superintendent at Port Harcourt, the centre of Nigeria's incipient oil industry.

"Aureol was a real step up for the company. After the first two postwar liners, Accra and Apapa, Elders realised they must up their game. Aureol was like a beautiful motor yacht, or a deluxe mini-cruise liner, probably the best looking ship ever to sail the Mersey."

SEA OF OPPORTUNITY

From dank basements to tropical voyages printer . . .

FED up with work in the dingy basement offices of small jobbing printers in Liverpool, a chance meeting with a union officer at Lime Street transformed 26-year-old Graham Austin's life.

"I was disillusioned and told the local printers' secretary to give us a shout if he heard anything interesting," said Graham, from Huyton.

"The next day he called and told me to report to the Elder Dempster Lines office in India Buildings. It was the best interview of my life.

"It went, 'Can you print?' I answered 'Yes!' and their response was 'You've got the job on the Aureol'."

In all, Graham made 42 round voyages working on Elder Dempster's flagship Aureol, including her last before withdrawal in October 1974. The six week round-trip liner service ran from Liverpool to Las Palmas (Canaries), Freetown (Sierra Leone), Monrovia (Liberia), Tema or Takoradi (Ghana), Lagos (Nigeria) and return.

"My predecessor on Aureol had died at sea off Liberia and other crew had struggled to keep the print room going," said Graham.

"Luckily, Aureol was docked in Liverpool for 11 days, but even then it took me one and a half voyages to sort the mess out.

"I am probably the last ships' printer to work out of Liverpool. The equipment they had on board was first class, totally different to the grotty stuff I worked with ashore. It was like being back in art college.

Graham Austin with his work from MV Aureol

"Twelve menus were needed each day for first class, cabin class and children, shipboard race meeting cards, constant cocktail party invitations, the ship's newspaper and stationery - it was all go.

"I loved the life. There was no humdrum journey to work, no fares to pay and the food was good. Aureol was a very happy ship.

Most of the men were married with kids and away for the six week round voyages.

"She was always a full ship going southbound, even on our last voyage. Passengers ranged from students to High Commission and colonial officials. Northbound would be a lot of Africans on contracts.

"I was never seasick, but sailing across the Irish Sea and the Bay of Biscay were the worse parts. Once you got to the Canaries it was very

m.v. "Aureol"
Captain D. Campbell

NIGERIAN INDEPENDENCE

1960 1972

ANNIVERSARY

Sunday 1 October 1972

Printed on Board

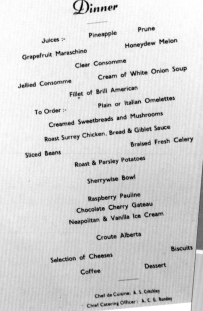

Dinner

Juices :- Pineapple Prune
Grapefruit Maraschino Honeydew Melon

Clear Consomme

Jellied Consomme Cream of White Onion Soup

Fillet of Brill American

To Order :- Plain or Italian Omelettes

Creamed Sweetbreads and Mushrooms

Roast Surrey Chicken, Bread & Giblet Sauce

Braised Fresh Celery

Sliced Beans

Roast & Parsley Potatoes

Sherrywise Bowl

Raspberry Pauline
Chocolate Cherry Gateau
Neapolitan & Vanilla Ice Cream

Croute Alberta

Selection of Cheeses Biscuits

Coffee Dessert

Chef de Cuisine: A. S. Critchley
Chief Catering Officer: A. C. G. Bunday

pleasant, but the tropical heat was bad. My printers' shop was next to the ship's laundry and it could get up to 100 °F."

The laundry men were from Sierra Leone as they tolerated the heat better than other races.

"There were some great British and African characters aboard and everyone got on - you had to for it to work smoothly," said Graham.

But the winds of changes were blowing. In 1972, Elder Dempster relocated Aureol to Southampton as Mersey Docks & Harbour Co wanted to close Princes Landing Stage as she was the only liner using it. From then on Liverpool crew were flown to Bournemouth and bussed to the liner. During the 1974 fuel crisis, Aureol's five days turnaround in port was cut to two days and the liner sailed at reduced speed of 14 knots instead of 16 knots to save fuel, creating slower voyages just as the airlines bit into passenger numbers.

"On the last voyage into Liverpool it was snowing and the dockers wanted extra 'snow' money to unload the baggage," said Graham.

"The passengers were stuck on the ship and had to be served lunch as the ship left Princes Landing Stage to berth in Brocklebank Dock where they disembarked. Not good.

"In March 1972, before the last voyage southbound, Langton Dock lock gate failed and Aureol had to move through the dock system and leave through Gladstone lock.

"Then she was trapped in thick fog, anchored off the stage. Luckily, I'd got on at midnight in Brocklebank Dock, but a lot of the crew had been waiting for six hours on the stage since 7am where we finally docked at 1pm.

"I spent four Christmases at sea, which at first I didn't look forward to, but they were the best I've ever had. Coastal mini-cruises from Lagos were hugely popular with ex-pats. Aureol would chug along on one engine so the other could be serviced while at sea."

Elder Dempster's MV Apapa on one of her last voyages on September 20, 1968

THE BURMA BOATS

VENERABLE

Bibby Line was founded in 1807 by John Bibby (1775–1840) and is Liverpool's last family-owned shipping line and possibly the world's oldest independent deep-sea line.

The current chief executive is Sir Michael Bibby, middle left, John Bibby's sixth generation descendant. He is with a model of Bibby Line's last troopship, SS Oxfordshire, of 1957, in the atrium of the company's head office at Duke Street, bottom left, flying the Bibby house flag.

Bibby ships are traditionally named after British counties and the 7,546 gross ton hospital ship SS Somersetshire ("I think we made that name up," said Sir Michael) is shown, top, bringing wounded troops home to Liverpool on VJ (Victory Over Japan) Day, August 15, 1945.

Above, Chistina Spencer, Bibby Line archivist, with Bibby passenger liner china and silverware displayed at Duke Street

VARIETY

That Bibby Line has out-lived almost all of its rivals is perhaps due to a willingness to diversify throughout its history with liner, cargo, floating hotel, foodstuff and financial services. Not only was it a conduit of the British Empire to Burma, with passenger and cargo services via Suez, between Birkenhead, Gibraltar, Marseille, Port Said, Port Sudan, Colombo and Rangoon, but also provided the government with peace time troopships. Although Burma (now Myanmar) gained independence from Britain in 1948, Bibby passenger services lasted to 1965.

Sir Michael Bibby said: "The Far East liner service was also promoted as a health- giving holiday cruise. But it must have got boring being stuck on a ship for so long, so from early on there were always attempts to jolly things up, as this postcard of a ladies' egg and spoon race on one of our ships in the early 1900s shows."

Top: Bibby Line cruise brochures from the 1930s; bottom: SS Staffordshire (I), 6,055 gross tons, loaded with Gordon Highlander troops destined for the Boer War, c1902

THE SUMMER EXODUS

HALCYON DAYS

The golden age of the British holiday is well illustrated here. Left, SS Manxman of the Isle of Man Steam Packet disgorges passengers from Douglas onto Princes Landing Stage. Above, St Seiriol, of Liverpool & North Wales SS Co loads for Llandudno and Menai Bridge – ahead is the IOMSP Company's Mona's Queen (both pictures from the late 1930s.) Below, IOMSP Company's SS Mona's Isle leaves the winter lay-up in Birkenhead on March 26, 1969, to be prepared for summer service

THE LOST GALLERY OF TREASURES

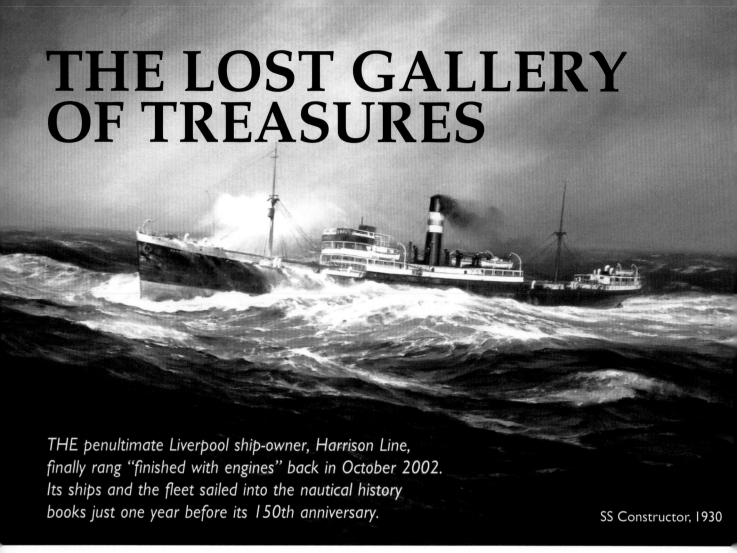

THE penultimate Liverpool ship-owner, Harrison Line, finally rang "finished with engines" back in October 2002. Its ships and the fleet sailed into the nautical history books just one year before its 150th anniversary.

SS Constructor, 1930

HOW ironic that Liverpool, the port that more than any other shrank the world, as its shipping line tentacles spread across the oceans, has so deeply suffered from the negative effects of the globalisation it set in motion.

No better illustration of the city's seismic change of direction is that of the Albert Dock, where Harrison's was the first tenant. The quay and warehouse where Harrison ships off-loaded Bordeaux wines and brandies from Charente, in France, is now occupied by the Italian restaurant Gusto.

The company's lineage begins in Liverpool's golden age. Thomas and James Harrison joined Samuel Brown in 1830 and became T & J Harrison. In 1871, Charente Ltd was founded and the Harrison brothers became the managers, using the name Harrison Line.

No more will the distinctive livery of red, white and black-banded funnels (which gave rise

to the quip "two of fat and one of lean" and thus the nickname "Hungry Harrisons") be seen on waters anywhere.

The ships, named after just about every profession except Anarchist or "the oldest one" have all been sold off.

Back in 2002, the atmosphere hung heavy in Harrison Line's Mersey Chambers head office, topped by the oldest Liver Bird statue in Liverpool.

Since the 1880s, this was the heart of a company – from where ships were ordered, men's lives directed and cargoes calculated – but it no longer beats. Enough remained to show you what a real shipping office should look like with 31 fabulous models, representing the fleet from the beginning, to the Wayfarer of 1973, all still gleaming within their shadowy glass cases. Magnificent paintings charting the company's course from sail to steam covered the

walls, including the Astronomer which served in the Falklands War and was eventually bought by the Ministry of Defence. Some of the older paintings, such as early 19th-century Merseyside examples by Joseph Hurd, Miles and Samuel Waters later fetched £20,000-£30,000.

Overlooking the Mersey's waters, the power and the glory still emanated from the boardroom's dark panelling, last officially used in April, 2002.

Yet it was up in the attic storey that the real soul, or memory of Harrison's lay. Here was a gallery of treasures, which covered the formal, ephemeral, quirky and serious that defined the character of one of Liverpool's greatest shipping lines. When the Harrison's office closed, Nigel Hollebone, Charente director, said: "Because we kept it all for ourselves there are cupboards stuffed with masses of detailed records: ship-building, crew lists, trade volumes and voyage details.

"Graeme Cubbins, a retired Harrison Line captain, built up the museum over the last couple of decades, besides writing the definitive history of the company. We've also got telescopes, tide clocks, chronometers, stability calculators to ensure you arrived the right way up after using all your fuel and water. They all have a value for collectors."

Books crammed with vital statistics give us the facts, but nothing conveys the lifeblood of a company like Harrison's as this marvellously jumbled set of artefacts. Merseyside Maritime Museum's chief, Mike Stammers, describes its record sections as: "The most complete history of any shipping line."

In spite of this endorsement, it was broken up and sold off with the rest. The most startling item looks inoffensive enough: a faded letter from the war years. Closer inspection reveals that it is a receipt signed by Capt Lansdorff, of the German pocket battleship, Graf Spee.

This was for a Harrison Line ship that he captured and used as a

Harrison's boardroom in Mersey Chambers; below, Hillman cars await loading on MV Inventor, and the 'third' Liver Bird, atop Mersey Chambers

larder for revictualling before sinking her. The receipt informs us that: "This ship is now a German prize."

Nigel Hollebone said: "I'm sure that, as a proper, well-ordered German he meticulously gave a receipt for every ship he sank. It meant the captain didn't get the sack for coming home empty-handed."

Photos showed the fast Harrison cargo-liner SS Politician which, due to compass error, was wrecked off a Scottish island while carrying £250,000 worth of whisky and bank notes.

The accident became the basis for Compton MacKenzie's novel and then Ealing Studios' comedy, Whisky Galore, with the ship renamed SS Cabinet Minister.

"There was a lot of talk that the captain was drunk, but he and the company were officially exonerated as the grounding was caused by magnetic variations caused by the Scottish islands," said Nigel Hollebone.

"Even to lose a ship in the war was not a fine thing. I suspect some of the Harrisons are still turning in their graves at the thought of all the publicity."

Between the wars, Harrison's ran a first class service, with the steamers Inkosi and Inanda, to the West Indies and carried the England Cricket Team to Trinidad. The company's zenith was just before WWII when the fleet numbered 48 ships.

After the postwar rebuilding programme the company had 41 ships in 1954. The last ship in the company's colours was the Author, on the Caribbean trade, which was highly popular with passengers wanting the long, leisurely voyages aboard a freighter.

Nigel Hollebone, who was with the company for 30 years, says: "The sale of the liner trades was sad but inevitable. We are competing with multi-national companies and its impossible to keep a toe in the water. We are a victim of the worldwide ➤

➤ consolidation into massive global alliances.

"Everyone understands it's inevitable that we should move away from liner services, particularly in this neck of the woods, where we have such a good name."

Charged with this task is Charente development director Peter Morton, who said: "We have to shrink the business to survive. We have two distinct businesses selling charts and making nautical instruments and compasses, plus ship-broking, which will continue from 1 Water Street, in Liverpool."

SEVEN STEPS TO HEAVEN

Harrison Line was so conservatively-minded, that, when they ordered their first post-war motor ship, it was delivered complete with all the crew's equipment for a coal-burning ship.

Pat Moran, one of the leading Merseyside maritime historians, says: "Harrisons was a very, very old-fashioned shipping line. The Harrisons were part of the Cumbrian ship-owning mafia who moved down the coast to Liverpool from Cockermouth. They built coal-burning ships until the beginning of the war – long after all the other big owners had switched to oil.

"When they ordered their first motor ship after the war, the captain, Harry Trainer, arrived to find it had come complete with rakes, barrows and slicers – no one had bothered to cancel the order for the equipment needed to look after the furnaces! First trippers aboard Harrison's ships were told that an island in the Indian Ocean, Secotra, I think, was called Harrison Island because so much clinker and ash had been dumped overboard there by its passing ships."

Harrison Line's ships were based at Birkenhead's Morter Mill Quay for East Africa, and Liverpool's Canada and Brunswick Docks for the West Indies and West Africa.

"The company was held in tremendous affection – more than any other shipping line – in Liverpool. After the war, it became known as a 'good feeder' for crews and even employed a dietician. Latterly, everyone on board could have steak.

"The company was a big supporter of the Sailors' Home, HMS Conway and HMS Indefatigable training establishments."

Harrison's was the only line that had its own pub, nicknamed 'The Seven Steps' in the Dock Road, near Brunswick Quay (now occupied by a graphics company). The crews were rounded up here for Friday night's sailings.

INDIAN SUMMER

Harrison Line's SS Dictator at Calcutta, in 1894, later sunk off Brazil, during the First World War, in September 1915. Harrison's distinctive black funnel with two white bands around a red one caused the nickname "two of fat and one of lean"

GOOD TIMES AND BAD

Laundry and galley crew aboard Harrison Line's MV Herdsman, in 1957. Above: Harrison's SS Politican, 8,100 gross tons in the Mersey, her grounding in fog on Eriskay, Outer Hebrides, and loaded with 28,000 cases of malt whisky in February, 1941, inspired Compton Mackenzie's 1947 novel Whisky Galore and the famous Ealing Studios film. Left: crates of whisky recovered from SS Politician's wreck

AMAZON ADVENTURE

THE Booth Steamship Co was founded by Alfred Booth and his younger brother Charles in 1866, running UK - Brazil services. In 1910-11 SS Stephen and SS Hildebrand were commissioned, described as a "mosquito-proof, electric ships". Navigating 1,000 miles up the Amazon to Manaus, Booth Line had one of the most exotic ocean shipping routes. In 1975 its ships were assimilated into Vestey's Blue Star and it ceased to exist as a separate entity.

Animals and exotic birds were the unofficial cargo on Booth Line's saintly-named ships like Hilary, Hubert and Hildebrand, always referred to as "Maggie Booth's" on Merseyside, which could have been a nickname for Mary Macauley, the philanthropic wife of Charles Booth.

Doug Sharkey was a young sailor who quickly grasped the potential of this trade. He joined SS Hilary as a scullion for a two-month trip in 1956, peeling potatoes and washing dishes, then transferred to the new Hubert.

"You could buy a parrot for a pound up the Amazon in a place called Manaus," Doug recalled in an interview with David Charters.

"You could sell them for £10 each when you got home. There was no problem buying them. Men came on board with them. When you got to Liverpool, the same thing applied. Someone came on board and bought them.

"Some made their own cages for them, but I was lucky. I had the potato lockers on the after-poop-deck. One was empty by the time we got to Manaus. On an average trip, I would take home about 15 parrots."

There could be as many as 200 parrots aboard. The seamen were paid about £19 a month, a fraction of their takings from the animal trade, but it was certainly not confined to them. Monkeys came in from Africa ➤

BOOTH LINE

TO PORTUGAL MADEIRA & NORTH BRAZIL

HILARY

CRUISES 1,000 MILES UP THE RIVER AMAZON

FOR TRAIN SERVICES, SEE L.N.E.R. TIME TABLES

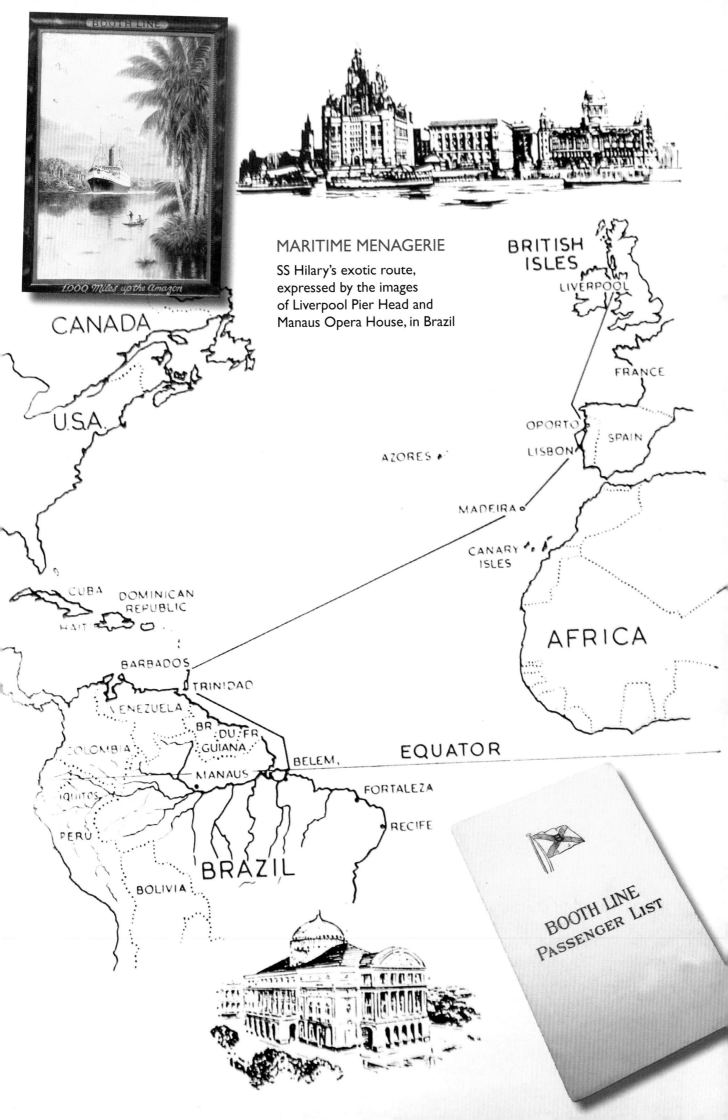

BOOTH LINE

1,000 Miles up the Amazon

MARITIME MENAGERIE

SS Hilary's exotic route,
expressed by the images
of Liverpool Pier Head and
Manaus Opera House, in Brazil

BRITISH ISLES

LIVERPOOL

FRANCE

OPORTO

LISBON

SPAIN

AZORES

MADEIRA

CANARY ISLES

AFRICA

CANADA

U.S.A.

CUBA

DOMINICAN REPUBLIC

HAITI

BARBADOS

TRINIDAD

VENEZUELA

BR DU FR GUIANA

COLOMBIA

BELEM

EQUATOR

MANAUS

IQUITOS

FORTALEZA

PERU

RECIFE

BRAZIL

BOLIVIA

BOOTH LINE
PASSENGER List

SS Hilary in the Mersey, with the stern of Alexandra's tug tender Flying Breeze ahead; below: Doug Sharkey

S.S. "HILARY."

➤ as well. Elder Dempster Line's ships travelling to and from west Africa were nicknamed "monkey boats".

Doug said: "We used to buy a sack of corn in Lisbon to feed the parrots. You had to be careful because they used to bite now and then and when they did you knew about it.

"We docked in the Kings Dock or the Queens Dock and the chap who bought them used to come on board. He had a big furniture van. He would pay you there and then, but you had to have a chitty from the Ministry of Agriculture, Fisheries and Food. The duty was two shillings (10p) per bird.

"In those days there was no trouble, though a bit later on, when the Customs got wise to it, they upped the duty and then there were these parrot diseases and they

put the blocks on it altogether."

It was easy to bring the monkeys and marmosets in as well. But there were restrictions on some animals, including jaguars and snakes, though it seems that these were also smuggled in.

Bush monkeys and marmosets were more likely to be personal

pets of the seamen. They were often allowed the run of the ship and could be seen playing in the rigging. The more considerate sailors made clothes for them. The ones who arrived safely in Liverpool would either be sold to pet dealers for about £10 each or kept by the families of the seamen.

Earlier, monkeys had played a part in the Battle of the Atlantic. With sharp senses, they were always aware of approaching ships, particularly enemy submarines, before the humans. They would show this by staring, motionlessly, in the direction of the coming danger.

"We had one fella who used to walk round with a monkey on his shoulder," says Doug, a father of three, who worked in the Vauxhall car factory, Ellesmere Port, after leaving the Merchant Navy in 1963.

Top left: a Booth liner steaming along the River Amazon; top right: SS Francis in Queens Graving Dock, Liverpool; bottom: Booth's new SS Hubert, 8,062 gross tons, built at Cammell Laird, Birkenhead, during speed trials on the Arran Mile, Firth of Clyde, in late 1954

FLAGGED UP

On a misty morning on August 14, 1931, two flat-capped spectators watch SS Hilary, 7,420 gross tons, pull away from Princes Landing Stage on her maiden voyage to Manaus, Brazil, via Leixoes/Oporto, Lisbon, Madeira, Barbados, Trinidad and Belem

"But I never fancied the monkeys after I got punched in the face by one in Manaus. He gave me a left hook. I'll tell you what, I felt it. They could bite as well.

"We had the big tortoises as well. Someone had found a market for them somewhere. On an average trip there would be a would be a couple of hundred parrots and about 30 monkeys. The captains weren't really happy about it, but in those days they turned a blind eye.

"I was pretty well off once I had sold the parrots, but you just went through the money in those days."

FUR & FEATHERS

It wasn't only the trade in parrots and monkeys which was known across the Port of Liverpool.

Pat Moran, a former Blue Funnel seafarer and maritime historian, said: "There is the story from a purser who said it was quite a surreal experience being in the next room to the bosun trying to convince the Customs man that the baby jaguar was a domestic cat which had wandered on board in Manaus.

"The jaguar was taken ashore and locked in a Customs' locker in a shed. The shore gang, who were good friends of the bosun, got into the locker during the night and took the jaguar out and up to a shop on Park Lane.

"The two mangiest cats they could find were put in the locker for the Customs to find the next morning. There might have been repercussions, but it was really a game. There were times when the crewmen won and times when Customs won. But it is true that very few men ever had to touch their wages. One chap had a three-toed sloth which he kept hanging in the paint locker."

On a very hot day in 1959 a harlequin mackaw became grumpy about being continually moved around the ship to keep him away from the authorities. These large birds had very strong hooked beaks which could crack open Brazil nuts.

"Anyway, this particular mackaw was fed up when a chap, wearing nothing underneath his boiler-suit, picked it up. The mackaw slid into his boiler suit and got hold of his wedding tackle. But they did get it out safely."

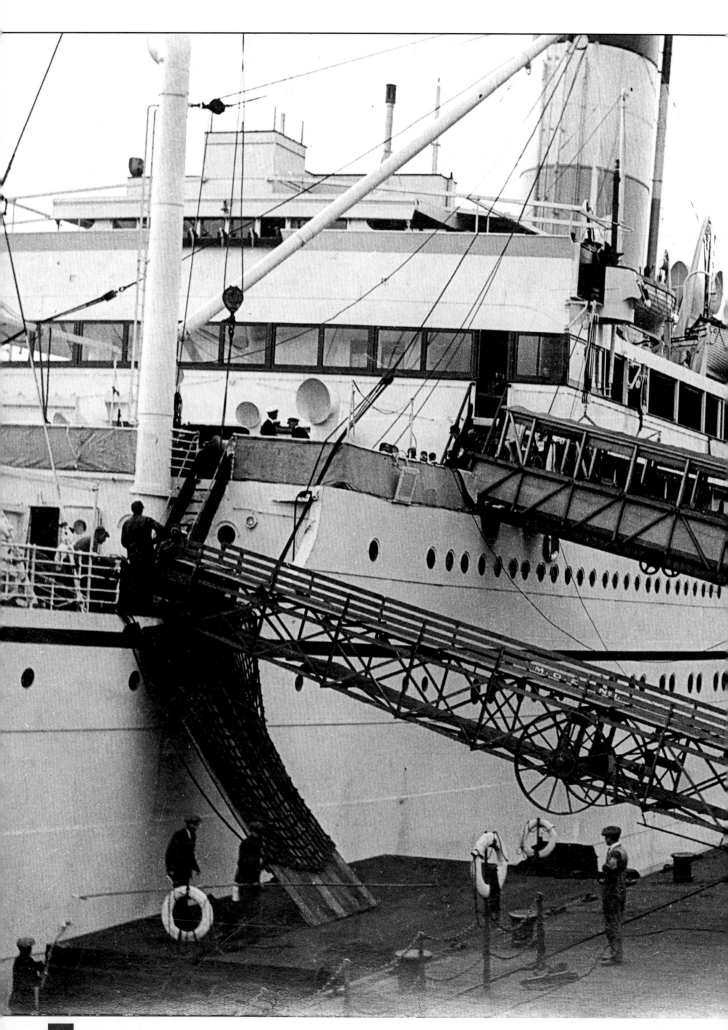

SS Voltaire, at the landing stage in the 1930s,
cruised to the Mediterranean, Atlantic Islands, West
Africa, West Indies, fjords and Baltic. She was sunk
by the German raider Thor on April 9, 1941

MADEIRA, M'DEAR?

A Walter Thomas poster, above,
of SS Voltaire, 13,248 gross tons,
at Funchal, to promote cruises
from 1932 by Lamport & Holt Line
to occupy its laid-up sister liners
Voltaire and Van Dyck. Left, Voltaire
loads cruise passengers at Princes
Landing Stage. Note the telescopic
gangways and Heath Robinson
style mobile luggage conveyor
(still used in the 1960s). Lamport
& Holt Line started in 1845, by
William Lamport (from Lancaster)
and George Holt, based at Fenwick
Buildings, Fenwick Street, Liverpool.
Lamport helped draft the first
Merchant Shipping Act, after
Samuel Plimsoll MPs demands for
better safety at sea

OUT OF AFRICA

MV Badagry Palm comes alongside Princes Landing Stage, on June 18, 1957, carrying Dr. Kwame Nkrumah, prime minister of Ghana, whose first comment was "It's hotter than in Ghana here." After lunch onboard with diplomats, he left from Liverpool Riverside Station by train to London for the Commonwealth Prime Minister's Conference. To the right, Alexandra's tug tender Flying Breeze is steaming away

BUSY BRUNSWICK

Top: Alexandra Towing Co's tugs bustle about Palm Line's three year old freighter, MV Badagry Palm, left, 7,275 gross tons, at Brunswick Dock entrance, Liverpool South Docks, in October 1959.

Left: Badagry Palm, in Gladstone Dock, during a strike in October, 1970. Palm Line, a former subsidiary of United Africa Co, traded with West Africa from 1949 until 1986, serving ports along the 5,000 mile coast from Morocco to Angola

REIGN OF THE WHITE EMPRESSES

Painters brighten up the hull of SS Empress of Britain, left, berthed in Gladstone Dock with her sister ship SS Empress of England, c1960

Ernie Ashley (pictured left in these two photographs) lived a life typical of so many Merseyside seafarers, moving between the famous fleets . . .

AFTER a catering course at the training ship Vindicatrix, at Sharpness, Gloucester, Ernie Ashley's first trip to sea was aged 16, in 1959, when he joined the Shell tanker Axina at Ellesmere Port – but that voyage to India and back lasted a year.

His life is typical of so many Merseyside seafarers, moving between the famous fleets.

"Although I was only at sea for 13 years, I have great memories of sailing out of Liverpool, mostly on Cunard, Canadian Pacific and Ellerman Lines," said Ernie, from Woolton.

During the mid-1960s, he was a steward aboard all three of Canadian Pacific's last 'white empresses' – Empress of Britain, Empress of England and Empress of Canada. Empress of Britain was his favourite.

"In summer we did the Liverpool – Montreal – Quebec liner service and in winter we sailed out of New York to the Caribbean," said Ernie.

"I was on Moss Hutchison's MV Memphis in 1962 and we did six week 'Medi' runs to Famagusta (Cyprus), Malta, Alexandria (Egypt) and Beirut (Lebanon) – a great run and happy days."

ANTI-DEPRESSION CRUISES

Between transatlantic voyages, Canadian Pacific's SS Montcalm, 16,418 gross tons, undertook cruises from Liverpool in the mid-1930s, seen on a glassy Mersey at Princes Landing Stage, with the bow of Lamport & Holt's SS Voltaire.
Opposite page, Canadian Pacific's brand new flagship, SS Empress of Canada, 27,284 gross tons, edges to the Landing Stage before her maiden voyage on April 24, 1961, with an Isle of Man Steam Packet turbine steamer already alongside

CANADIAN PACIFIC

Express Steamship and Railway Services.

TO CANADA AND U.S.A.

From Liverpool, Southampton, Glasgow, Belfast, Queenstown, Hamburg. Antwerp, Cherbourg, to Quebec and Montreal (in Summer), and St. John, N.B. (in Winter).

ACROSS CANADA

To Vancouver from Montreal in ninety hours ; from Toronto in eighty-six hours.

TO JAPAN AND CHINA

By the largest and fastest ships on the Pacific from Vancouver.

THROUGH BOOKINGS TO NEW ZEALAND AND AUSTRALIA

IMPERIOUS

The glowing new SS Empress of Britain (III), 25,516
gross tons, of 1956, berthed at Princes Landing Stage,
seen from a Mersey ferry in the late 1950s

Liverpool's last three funnelled liner, the magnificent SS Empress of
Scotland, 26,313 gross tons, which first set sail from Liverpool for
trans-Pacific service on June 14, 1930 (withdrawn 1957), approaching
the stage, with fireboat William Gregson berthed in front

Empress of Canada (III) anchored mid-river for lifeboat drill with Cock tugs Pea Cock and Fighting Cock at the stage in this richly-textured Stephen Shakeshaft photograph, of August, 1966

STEAMING OFF TO SOUTH AMERICA

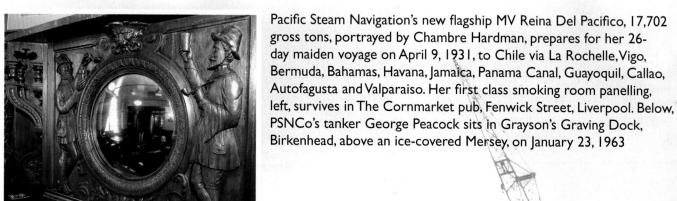

Pacific Steam Navigation's new flagship MV Reina Del Pacifico, 17,702 gross tons, portrayed by Chambre Hardman, prepares for her 26-day maiden voyage on April 9, 1931, to Chile via La Rochelle, Vigo, Bermuda, Bahamas, Havana, Jamaica, Panama Canal, Guayoquil, Callao, Autofagusta and Valparaiso. Her first class smoking room panelling, left, survives in The Cornmarket pub, Fenwick Street, Liverpool. Below, PSNCo's tanker George Peacock sits in Grayson's Graving Dock, Birkenhead, above an ice-covered Mersey, on January 23, 1963

IDEAL SUNSHINE TOUR ROUND

SOUTH AMERICA
ROBINSON CRUSOE'S ISLAND
& WEST INDIES

The Sunshine Ship M.V. "REINA DEL PACIFICO" 17707 TONS
From LIVERPOOL 10th JAN. 1940

PACIFIC LINE

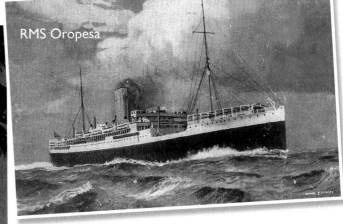

RMS Oropesa

LATIN LINE

Eileen Lloyd's grandmother, Lucy Richardson (pictured below c1928), didn't need to be empowered by Women's Lib to take off and get on a boat to South America.

Even having five children and a husband didn't stop her. Against her husband's wishes, she joined Cammell Laird's office staff to "do her bit" in WWI, cycling eight miles a day to work.

"That must have given her 'itchy feet', as in September 1920, she became a stewardess on Pacific Steam Navigation's RMS Oropesa, leaving my mother, aged 15, to tend to an older brother and three young siblings," said Eileen, of Neston, Wirral.

"I know she knocked five years off her age to join. I have her discharge books and in 1923 for a voyage on RMS Orcoma from Liverpool to west coast South America she was paid £9.25p a month, with 7/7d National Insurance (40p) and four shillings (20p) health insurance.

"I wish I'd asked her more about her travels before she passed away in 1962, but when young one doesn't think of the past, only the future."

LIVERPOOL

PACIFIC LINE R.M.S. "ORTEGA," August 17, 1926

MENU DU DINER

Chilled Spanish Melon

Hors d'Œuvres Variés

Consommé Caroline   Potage Mulligatawny

Grilled Haddock, Sauce Crevette

Arroz Valenciana   Asperges, Sauce Mousseline
Paupiettes de Bœuf aux Olives

Roast Leg of English Pork, Savoury & Apple Sauce

Dinde Braise, Sauce Chipolata

Pommes de Terre Bouillies et Rôties
Carottes Française   Haricots Verts

BUFFET FROID :-
Jambon de York   Aloyau de Bœuf
Salade Naturale

Patisserie Assortie
Pouding Diplomat
Glacé Française et Gauferettes

Tortillas Español

Fromage   Dessert   Café

FRUITFUL CRUISING THROUGH THE 1970s

Aznar Line's express fruit and passenger liner MV Monte Anaga, 6,813 gross tons, running mate to Monte Umbe, berthed in Queens Dock, Liverpool South Docks, on February 16, 1972, with St John's Beacon poking above her bow. Right, Eileen Taylor

LIVERPOOL TO THE SUN

AZNAR LINE to the Canary Islands

Going bananas for Aznar Line . . .

THEY were called the "Banana Boat Cruises", but were highly popular with passengers, recalls Eileen Taylor.

The boats in question were owned by Aznar Line and ran a service between Liverpool, the Canary Islands and Spain. This was marketed as a two week cruise from Liverpool to La Coruna, Tenerife, Las Palmas, Madeira, Vigo and back - still popular today with Cruise & Maritime Voyages (Newmarket Holidays) and Fred Olsen Cruise Lines.

The Spanish-owned ships were express fruit carriers to transport mainly bananas and tomatoes to the UK.

But their Merseyside and North Wales passengers found a cruise trip on Aznar's Monte Anaga, Monte Umbe and Monte Granada a welcome break from the UK's grim mid-1970s' economic recession.

"They were a far cry from today's big cruise liners," said Eileen Taylor.

"The ships were homely, rather than glamorous, and very friendly. People loved them."

Eileen worked for Kershaw PR, in Liverpool, which handled publicity for Aznar Line and Yeoward Bros, the famous fruit importers.

She took a Canary Islands round trip with her seven-year-old son Mark from Liverpool, in August, 1974.

"We sailed on the Monte Umbe, which carried 361 passengers in one class. The food was simple, but good - more like a boarding house than a hotel!

"We shared a table for four with a North Wales' couple. It wasn't just retired couples, there were families aboard, too.

"Monte Umbe was a bit of an old tub, but our cabin had a porthole and en suite facilities. No balcony, TV or radio in those days. ➤

➤ "There was a small square swimming pool on deck, which kept Mark and the other children happy.

"But it was really just the ship and the sea. There weren't any sun-loungers, just slatted wooden seats, like a Mersey ferry.

"It was a lovely, old-fashioned cruise, no loud entertainment, but many people prefer that kind of gentle holiday at sea.

"The Bay of Biscay was a bit grey and choppy, but after that it was sunshine all the way. The weather was fantastic," recalls ileen.

"I remember it was 100'F at Lanzarote and we took a taxi to the beach. We went sight-seeing at each port, Madeira was especially lovely, and I think all the tours were free - which you certainly wouldn't get now.

"They were great days. My boss, Gordon Kerr, the people from Aznar Line and Yeoward Bros, were all a pleasure to work for."

STRANDED

Monte Anaga aground near Brazil Buoy,
New Brighton – as is Rea's rescue tug
Maplegarth, on July 16, 1969

OCEAN WAVE

Passengers about to
leave on MV Monte
Anaga, on July 30, 1969.
Right, Monte Anaga
unloads cargo at Kings
Dock, September, 1968

CRUISING LARKS FROM LIVERPOOL

Used to the stately transatlantic run, former Cunard Line purser John Shepherd was suddenly catapulted into running the morning deck hikes and calling the evening bingo when the company's ships were switched to cruising...

BACK in the late 1960s, passengers were deserting ocean liner travel for the airlines and Cunard was desperate to redeploy its liners built for the North American services.

"These were the pioneering days of cruising from Liverpool. You could describe it like Dickens, 'What larks, Pip! What larks!'," says former ship's purser John Shepherd, of Wallasey, who runs website www.liverpoolships.org.

"Cunard, Canadian Pacific and Lamport & Holt all ran very successful pre-war cruises from Liverpool, marketed as 'a guinea a day' (or £1.05p today), but the war put a stop to that.

"Then there was a long gap until December 1966 when we took Carinthia on a Christmas and New Year cruise to the Atlantic Islands.

"We only carried 550 passengers, rather than the usual 900 on the transatlantic runs. A seven person entertainment team was put onboard for the cruises.

"Even though it was early days, we looked after the passengers really well on our liners, Carinthia and Sylvania. The décor and accommodation was very attractive.

"The crew was pretty good. Thomas Cook organised all the shore tours. Both ships had cinemas with a new film every day.

"Cunard catering was superb in first class and really good in second. There was 98 per

Cunard's liner RMS Sylvania, right, handles cargo at Gladstone Dock, while on the New York run, with freighter MV Ivernia is left. Bill Harrison (pictured left with guitar) was with Cunard Line in the 1950s. He recalled: "Some of the records we brought back we sold to Brian Epstein's brother, Clive, for the first Epstein music shop. Girls would get hold of a copy of the Shipping News, and they'd see what ships were coming in and go down to the Locarno for the dance."

cent satisfaction and very few complaints.

"The problem was that these ships were essentially emigrant carriers and had very limited en suite cabin facilities, which even then was old-fashioned.

"The other problem was that, designed for the North Atlantic run, they only had air conditioning in the main public rooms. In hot climes, the crew used to take their mattresses and sleep in the tourist restaurant.

God knows what it smelt like at breakfast! I recall a 35-day West Indies cruise on Sylvania in 1967 and by the time we reached Trinidad we were all frying.

"Some passengers left the ship of their own accord and flew home! The classic Liverpool cruise was and is a two week itinerary to Madeira, Tenerife, Casablanca, Gibraltar and Lisbon.

"Very occasionally we went to the eastern Mediterranean, as far as Haifa, in Israel. Bizarrely,

in winter it always seemed to be snowing in Athens and Istanbul.

"The Med can be pretty foul in March and April. Once, Sylvania steamed around Malta four times as it was too rough to enter Valletta. We pressed on to Cyprus, which was one of my worst nights at sea."

The very last Cunard cruises from Liverpool were run by Franconia, which ran Cunard Line's last scheduled services from Liverpool in January, 1968.

Workmen fit a 19ft wide bronze propeller to Cunard's new Mauretania (II)
in Gladstone Graving Dock, 1939

THE SHIP BEAUTIFUL

Aptly illustrating her nickname, with her subtle sheer and perfect proportions, RMS Aquitania, 45,647 gross tons, starts her maiden voyage on May 20, 1914, to Queenstown (Cobh) and New York, watched by crowds on Princes Landing Stage.

What should have been a triumph for Cunard Line was a very muted event due to the horrific sinking of Canadian Pacific's Empress of Ireland a day before with 1,012 people killed.

Charlie Sutherland, former Cunard purser, from north Liverpool, recalled the late 1940s' final years of "the Aqui", carrying war brides to Halifax, Nova Scotia.

He said: "By then, Cunard didn't want to spend any money on her. If something broke, it stayed broke.

"The ship was packed with war brides, even on winter crossings. We tried to get some to help in the purser's office, but they kept being sea sick into the typewriters so that was no use.

"One very time-consuming task was compiling lists of the women's religious denominations to forward to their new parishes in Canada.

Once, to speed things up, the senior purser decided, rather than ask directly, to put CoE by English sounding surnames, Methodist by Scottish ones, Roman Catholic by Irish ones and Presbyterian by Welsh ones.

"The result was that soon Roman Catholic priests were calling on red-hot Orange Lodgers and so on. There was a hell of a row, but we were never found out!"

ALL ABOARD CUNARD FOR CANADA

The new Carinthia leaves John Brown Yard at Clydebank in Scotland in 195[...]

Arguably the world's most famous shipping company, Cunard Line was founded in Liverpool in 1840, by a Canadian, Samuel Cunard, after winning the Royal Mail transatlantic contract. Relocated south in 1966, it remains a premier part of Carnival Corp's cruise operation.

WHAT was it like to sail the Atlantic? John Shepherd, a former Cunard Line purser, says working aboard the liners was among his happiest times.

"I sailed as crew purser on the RMS Carinthia throughout 1964 and 1965, until the seamen's strike of May,1966. After a spell on the original RMS Queen Mary, I joined RMS Sylvania for 1967 as senior assistant purser.

"The Cunard berth at Liverpool was Huskisson Dock, and Carinthia would be towed to anchor in the Mersey until moving alongside the stage to embark passengers at 4pm.

"Sailing day on the Canadian service was always Wednesday 8pm,and Carinthia would be back in the Mersey at about 6am, 16 days later (a Friday).

"The crew purser's office-a space no bigger than 10 feet by six feet - was always a tremendous hive of activity as soon as Carinthia berthed on the stage on sailing afternoon."

There was always a fierce loyalty

Flying Scotsman is swung aboard Saxonia – courtesy of the Mersey Docks & Harbour Board floating crane Mammoth – bound for the US, on September 19, 1969

among the crews of the Carinthia and Sylvania. They were 95% Merseysiders compared with the new QM2, which carries more than 80% foreign nationals in her crew.

John said: "Sailing time was always very sad. At least 60% of the passengers would be emigrants to Canada, leaving the UK for probably the last time.

"There were many emotional farewells outside the tourist purser's office as final goodbyes were said and visitors were urged to go ashore. Carinthia's master in the early 1960s was Captain R J N Nicholas, who lived in Elmpark Road, Wallasey. There were always

three mighty blasts on the steam whistle when Carinthia passed New Brighton for the benefit of Mr Nicholas and their three dogs - but mainly for the dogs!

"You always thought there would be Cunarders at Liverpool. Life on Carinthia and Sylvania in the early to mid-1960s seemed as if it had no end, although the writing was on the wall. Jet travel was fast taking over.

"The former Deputy Prime Minister John Prescott's 1966 seamens' strike was the catalyst (but not the only cause) of these two fine ships' withdrawal at the end of 1967."

THE MAURY'S YOUNGEST PROJECTIONIST

Alfred Mahon never expected ever to see again the lonely young boy whom he befriended to help him run the cinema onboard the liner Mauretania in 1953.

Now nearly 60 years later, that 11-year-old passenger, Michael Ewer, whom the 19-year-old chief petty officer Alf made "probationary projectionist" on the Cunard liner, tracked him down to his Wallasey home. Mike, aged 70, is now professor of cardiology at the University of Texas in Houston, USA.

But he never forgot Alf's kind gesture and the thrill of running the ship's cinema on a five-day summer voyage from New York six decades ago.

Through the internet he found a letter Alf wrote to the ECHO about galley boys throwing dirty crockery overboard. Alf said: "I then received this letter from Mike asking if he could come over to visit. I was absolutely amazed. I didn't sleep that night. It was fantastic to see him."

Mike wrote in his letter: "I hope you will remember me after all these years. I was travelling with my grandfather on Mauretania on June 20, 1953, from New York.

"You made a tremendous impact on my life. I went to medical school, but before that I earned a projectionist's certificate in 1960."

Alf said: "Mike was tremendous. He had a mind like a sponge and learned everything I taught him about the films, Peter Pan and A Queen Is Crowned. He can still say how fast the film ran."

Top, a young Alf Mahon, onboard Mauretania while cruising. Above, Mauretania approaching the stage. Right, Mike Ewer and Alf Mahon, far right

CUNARD QUALITY

Top, Cunard Line's stupendous 1914 "palazzo" style headquarters, showing the Water Street entrance, taken by Colin Lane from the adjacent Royal Liver Building, home to Canadian Pacific. Above left, the Cunard boardroom in which the first three Queen liners were conceived. Right, a keystone carved as one of Columbus' galleons

VISIT AMERICA

CUNARD WHITE STAR

WHITE STAR LINE

SERVICES TO ALL PARTS OF
THE WORLD

White Star Line's berths at Gladstone Dock. Above, a poster
produced after the merger of rivals Cunard and White Star in 1934

ACROSS THE WORLD

Above, emigrants for Australia get a pep-talk from the Future Emigrants To Australia Society officials aboard Cunard White Star's MV Georgic, 27,759 gross tons, at Princes Landing Stage, on April 8, 1949. Below, MV Britannic (Georgic's sister ship), left, and RMS Lancastria, far right, sail on the tide from the Stage, in this Chambre Hardman picture from the late 1930s. Cunard's tender SS Skirmisher, front, heads back to the stage

CASE STUDY

Top, a well-wrapped schoolboy admires the model of RMS Mauretania (I) in the Cunard Building, in February, 1956. Above, Mauretania (I) herself, 31,938 gross tons, moves through Sandon Dock. Left, former Cunard steward and ex-deputy prime minister Lord (John) Prescott locates his former crew cabin on a model of Mauretania (II) at Merseyside Maritime Museum

Cunard's Sylvania, left, and Canadian Pacific's Empress of Britain load passengers at Princes Landing Stage for New York and Canada, respectively, on Friday, 13 January, 1961

Anchor-Donaldson Line's SS Athenia, in the Mersey, was the first loss of WWII, sunk in-bound from Canada, in September, 1939

5

ON LAND AND SEA

White Star Line's former James Street/ Strand HQ, bought by Pacific Steam Navigation – hence the foyer floor mosaic of South America

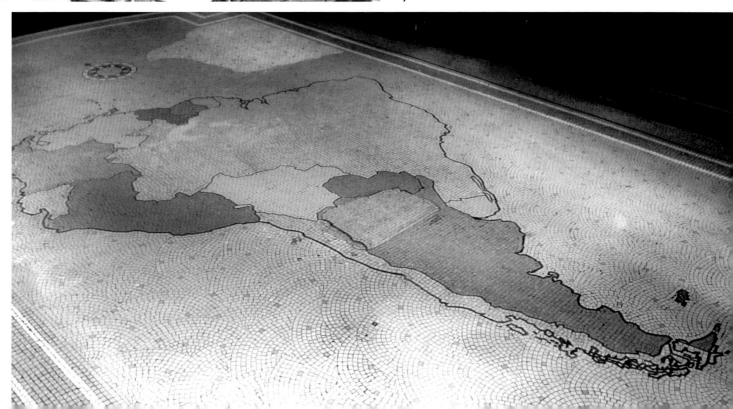

Mauretania (II), 35,674 gross tons, seen from her crow's nest, while being refitted in Gladstone Graving Dock, December, 1957

Franconia, 21,717 gross tons, made Cunard's last scheduled sailing from Liverpool, on January 30, 1968

TOP GALLANTS

Coronation Day of June 2, 1952, remains a vivid memory for Mike Davies, of Southport. He worked in the Balmoral Restaurant of Cunard Line's RMS Caronia, which acted as a floating five-star hotel for super-rich Americans in Southampton Docks.

Back then, said Mike, Caronia (dubbed "the Green Goddess" after her heat reflective paint scheme and Liverpool's trams) was the world's most luxurious liner – "the creme de la creme". He recalled: "London hotels were booked up long in advance, so the bed shortage was resolved by Caronia doing a Coronation cruise with four days in Southampton. We then went into refit and the passengers, who were superb guests, returned to New York on the Queen liners."

Mike, who started as a boy rating, aged 16, said: "We left Liverpool for New York in November, 1951, did four West Indies cruises, an Africa-India, a Mediterranean and Coronation cruises. It was before the transatlantic airlines got going and the liners were packed. Nothing could touch Caronia for quality." Pictured above, RMS Caronia, awaits dry-docking in Gladstone Dock, on her maiden visit in 1947.

COME, evening sunlight, warmth of womb,
Flood into my sitting room,
Flood across the western sea,
And stir a Pilot's memory.
Take me back to Lynas Point,
(My trencher fill, my glass anoint),
And let me tell thee of the scene,
On many a balmy summer's e'en,
When liners, as their trade they plied,
Came handsomely and on the tide,
For Liverpool, from lands enchanted,
And how men took it all for granted.

See you first the grand Cunard,
With New York mail-flag at her yard:
The CPR next from Quebec,
The icy-scheduled, foggy trek.
A Clan Line steamer from Ceylon,
An Ellerman from Lebanon,
A BP Tanker from Iran,
And here's Blue Funnel from Japan.
From Panama comes NZS,
Home from Auckland, wool-express,
And in her wake Shaw Savill who is
Home from Sydney, via Suez.

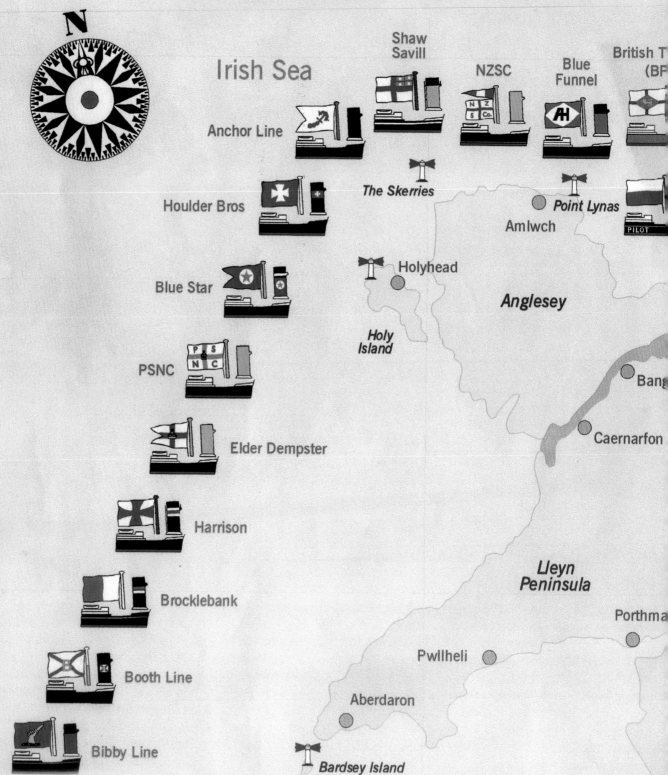

An Anchor Liner from Bombay,
A Houlder boat from Uruguay,
Blue Star with Argentinian cargo,
And PSN from Santiago,
An Elder Dempster from Accra,
A Harrison from Zanzibar,
A Brocklebank with tea, Madras,
Intrepid Booth Line from Manaus.
The sun, it will be setting soon;
Ah, here comes Bibby from Rangoon.
Each takes her Pilot from the Cutter,
A routine matter, bread and butter.

What panorama was afforded!
...All in the daily log recorded.

So, darling children at my knee,
It was a wondrous life,
D'you see?

by Barrie Youde
Illustration by
Garry Gannicliffe

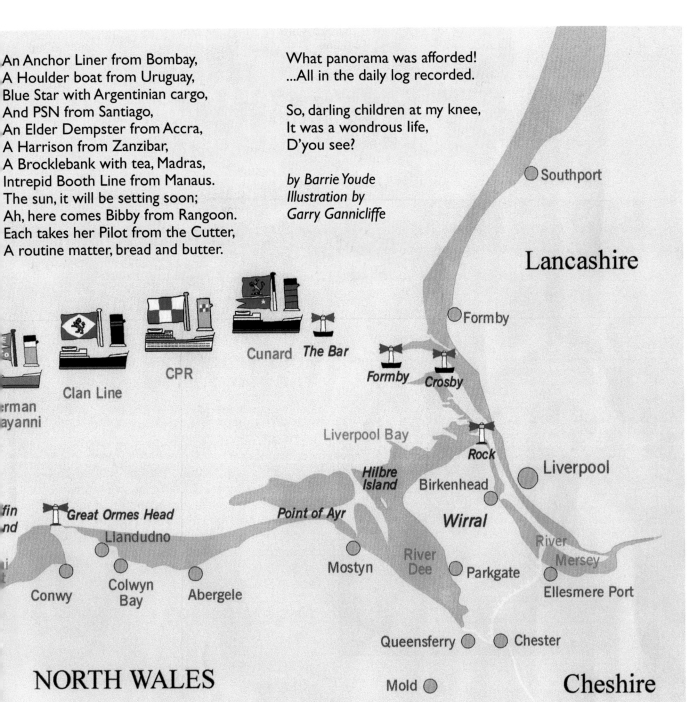

DISTANCES TO LIVERPOOL IN NAUTICAL MILES

New York (USA)	3074	Bombay (India)	6227
Quebec (Canada)	2626	Montevideo (Uruguay)	6123
Colombo (Ceylon/Sri Lanka)	6662	Buenos Aires (Argentina)	6241
Beirut (Lebanon)	3267	Valparaiso (Chile)	7191
Abadan (Iran)	6547	Accra (Ghana)	3847
Yokohama (Japan)	11104	Zanzibar (Tanzania)	6277
Panama (Panama)	4571	Madras (India)	7225
Auckland (New Zealand)	11176	Manaus (Brazil)	4905
Sydney (Australia)	11488	Rangoon (Burma)	7892
Suez (Egypt)	3255	Point Lynas (Anglesey)	52

© LAVER publishing 2003 / Barrie Youde 2002

WHEN HAPPINESS COST NOTHING...

The long-awaited follow up to 'The Lost Tribe of Everton & Scottie Road'

LOST TRIBE THE PEOPLE'S MEMORIES

IN the long-awaited follow up to the best-selling book, 'The Lost Tribe of Everton & Scottie Road', author Ken Rogers once again takes you on a journey into Liverpool's inner city terraced streets, questioning whether the 1960s 'clearances' of Everton and Scotland Road, that affected over 125,000 people, were absolutely necessary.

This new book provides a catalogue of fascinating memories from the people who, like the author, lived in those steep streets of Everton and the inner city heartland area of Scotland Road.

ONLY £7.50

PLUS £1 P&P UK

SAVE 25%
RRP £9.99

eBOOK ALSO AVAILABLE FROM AMAZON AND THE iBOOK STORE

VISIT WWW.LOSTTRIBEOFEVERTON.COM TO VIEW PHOTOGRAPHS AND LEAVE YOUR OWN TRIBUTES AND MEMORIES